A Bit Of Truth

BY

BUFORD L. HORNER

ISBN: 0-75963-781-4

This book is printed on acid free paper.

1stBooks - rev. 6/29/01

A Collection of rhymes dedicated to

my family and friends.

AUTHOR'S NOTES

Little rhymes written over a period of two years,

thoughts about truth and fiction that rhyme.

Read and find A Bit Of Truth.

Some of these poems have been published in the book

Memories and Daydreams

Everlasting Dreams

Poetic Voice of America

Aspiration of Pen and Thought

Sound of Poetry

America the Millennium

A few on poetry.com

Orange County, VA. News

ACKNOWLEDGMENT

I would like to mention with special gratitude:

Loretta Kfoury for her friendship and help with the typing. Nicky Horner for his advice and typing instructions. Linda & Ken Bishop for their friendship and putting my work in order.

TABLE OF CONTENTS

BABIES

Babies they come one, two, three,
four, five, six, seven, and sometimes eight.
Baby girls and baby boys, they come.
You give them names and you buy them toys.
They grow. You grow.
You watch them learn to walk,
you watch them learn to talk and they come.
Now big girls and boys still they come.

THE HOBOS RIDE TO THE SUN

Just sitting here in the park.

It looks like it will snow.

I hear that tonight it will be zero.

It's beginning to rain, I think I hear sleet.

Tonight will be cold.

This cardboard box doesn't have any heat.

It would be nice to be where it is warm.

I think of Florida and all that sun.

I can't hitch a ride and I have no cash.

I see the hobos running fast, they are headed for the train that is going past.

I've got an idea how to get out of here.

I pick up my bag and begin to run to catch the train to the Florida sun.

THE RACE IS ON

The race is on through the
bush and through the grass.
Some going slow,
some going fast.
They make their turns with
great ease. You would never guess
they could with all that speed.
The hooves fly, they jump high,
faster, faster they really try.
The riders feel great.
They've done their best.
They pushed to win.
They didn't hold to ride like that,

you must be bold.

As they came into the homestretch,

the cameras flashed, and the people screamed.

“There’s my winner, I’ve got my dream”.

DANCE

The music plays and we dance.

Dance in the crowd, dance alone.

Dance all day, dance all night.

Dance in the moon and the morning light.

Dance while the sun is shining,

snow is blowing, the rain is falling.

We dance.

HORSE

Horse is his name,
he is tall, long and
he is lean.
He is not gentle. He is
not mean. He is a little
something in between.
He is fun. He is my pet,
he loves to run when I say get.
He runs like a breeze
until I say come and he
comes to me like a native son.
Horse is fun, yes, Horse is fun.

PROMISE OF THE RAINBOW

The rainbow gives a promise
after the storm and after the rain.
The earth is calm and the birds sing.
The rainbow in all of its color
gives promise of a beautiful day
as the men work and the children play.
To the end I would like to go, to
check its colors and its bow, to
see if what I have been told
that at the end there's a pot of gold.

HUNT

We beat our drums until
morning comes, now to the
hunt everyone.
The wolves cry, the bows
fly. The deer fall, something
must die.
Our people must eat. We
live off the land, we hunt
animals not raised by man.
We are hunters, it must have
been God's plan. Something
must die.

BOAST

His job takes him from coast to coast, but
how he does boast about how much
everything cost and how much he is paid.
He has it made in the shade. He is
storing some away for a rainy day, when
he is old and he doesn't receive any pay.
He boast about how he works and
how he saves. He knows he can't take
it with him to the grave, but likes a little
cash stashed away.
He would like to leave some cash for
his brother and a few others when he goes.
When that day comes, sing a song and

spread his ashes along the coast. He
hates to boast but he has already paid.

THE OLD HOUSE AND THE OLD MILL

Along the road
and at the top of the hill;
the chimney tops you can see,
peeping up from behind the
trees so many houses where
the farms used to be.
The old mill goes around
and around, no more wheat or corn
to grind, just one of the sights
you will see, along the road at
the top of the hill.

1950'S DATE

One little kiss goodnight
and he was on his way. I
knew I would see him
another day.
That day came, we had a
great time. I couldn't go to
his place, he couldn't go
to mine.
Movies we enjoyed and
a little snack from the diner
that we ate in the car. We
would ride in the country,
we didn't go far.

We worked and we played
but, we drifted apart. I wish
him the best, my old
sweetheart.

WINNER

Winner do you know who you are?

Did you win a jackpot? Did you win a car?

Do you have good health? Do you

have good friends? Do you want

your days to be long or do you wish

for them to end?

Do you have romance? Do you

wine, dine, and dance? Are you

afraid to take a chance, your life to enhance?

It doesn't matter about any of the

above, the winner is the one that

chooses love.

THE DOOR IS OPEN

The door is open, come in friend. I'm glad to see you. Where have you been? Did you travel far? Did you go by train or did you go by car? I would guess you flew, just look at you.

Are you glad to be home? Talk to me, throw me a bone. Did you see big cities and the countryside? Did you see the oceans and the mountains high? It has been a long time, there is lots I want to know. Come in friend, tell me about all the places you have been, the people that you have met and all the in between, all the things that you have laughed and cried about,

don't leave anything out. The door is open.

Come in friend.

THE GRASS AND THE SUN

Paint everywhere, some solid and some
striped, paint splattered all about, you will
have to ask the painter what it means.
He is a master in his mind, just one of a kind
but he knows that you would like a scene so
he will paint you something in green.
He painted the scene green, he added some
blue and a little yellow, too.
He splatters on some white.
He stands gazing at his work, he said very
proud, “I painted the scene, it’s not all green,
I painted it for you, I call it the
Grass and the Sun.”

JOY

I find joy in my work and in my play,
the flowing brook that flows my way.
Joy in the sunshine and in the rain,
I find joy in many things.
Joy of a new birth, if it be boy, girl or both.
Joy in music and reading a book,
working in my garden or being a cook.
Joy with my friends as they come and go,
the special ones when we go to the picture show.
Joy hearing the birds singing in the birch,
joy singing in the choir at church.
Joy in God when I talk to him in prayer,
I find joy everywhere.

MY LITTLE MAN'S JOURNEY

Where are you going my son with that pack upon your back? Do you have a map to help you find your way, or will you follow the sun?

You've grown so big, it seems like only yesterday you were my little one.

Call me son. I will give you a dime. I know you will be busy, you've got mountains to climb.

Don't go alone, take friends; it's nice to travel with a few good men.

When your journey's done, come on home, bring your friends and your pack. I will be here to welcome you back.

MOVE THE PEOPLE

They were torn from their land
they were the mountain people
living where the National Park
now stands.
The government came with
their papers forcing them from
their homes, not just some but,
everyone must move on.
They moved what they had, the
good and bad, leaving the
only home that they had known.
They still talk today about their
land that was taken away and the

tales you hear about those mountains,
their school and their missions.
In the spring, some farming and some
fishing, in the winter the snow so deep
the one room school with its wood heat.
They talk about things one shouldn't
know, who shot Bill Joe, the moonshine
made for medicine, and whose wife left
with the Reverend Hearsayson - on, and on
they go, but not back to the mountain.

SCHOOL IS OUT

School is out, summertime is here.
You will play and run about, ride
your bike and fish for trout, what a
wonderful time of year.
Play with your cars and other toys, invite
all the girls and boys; have a party.
Do your chores, tomorrow you can play
out of doors. Put your toys in their box,
pick up your dirty socks.
Take your bath and say your prayers.
I will read you a story about The Three Bears.
Tomorrow you can sleep late. School is out.
Celebrate.

THE NEED TO HUNT

Winter has come, the snow is cold.
We must hunt more deer and buffalo,
some to trade, some to eat, skins to
keep out the cold and to keep in the heat.
The campfire is ablaze as the drums we beat
low. The moon beams its light on the cold
snow. My papoose is asleep in the teepee.
I know she is depending on me.
I put my ear to the ground. I hear the herd
moving around. Now we know where to hunt,
we will be on our way before the sun comes up.

PLAYING OUT OF DOORS

The rain is warm and sometimes cool,
when the rain comes fast, it makes a big pool,
but the pool dries and a rainbow appears.
What a lovely sight a sky so clear.
We play outside in the sun,
playing ball – run, run.
We slide in the mud and made a big splash.
We play and play, but not on the grass.
We play football; we make a pass.
The game is over; we win at last,
but look at us we are a mess.
We should have played on the grass.
Mother comes out with the garden hose.

We weren’t suppose to get mud on our clothes.

Mother sings the wash day blues

as the water flows.

LET US MOVE

Out of Heaven

out of the sky

the Hale-Bopp

Comet, you can

see it clear.

Hale and Bopp

observed the bright

light as it appeared.

They reported the sight

on a July night in 1995.

They kept observing as

it moved. The group from

Heavens Gate said, "Let us

get ready for it's time for us to go."

They were to hitch a ride on the UFO. They were going to meet Peep, Doe said so.

They were to move into another space and another time. The news reported thirty-nine had died. They were dressed, their bags by their side, waiting for a ride.

IT'S LONELY HERE

She was rocking in her rocking chair,
her hair so white and her eye sight
dim. She was lonely as she rocked,
she heard a voice very clear, saying,
"Hello dear, hello dear."
She said, "Hello love. Is that you?
I've been sitting here thinking of you.
I've missed you love. You've been
gone a long time."
She heard him answer, "I was walking in
the garden, I thought you would be there.
Please come out for awhile?"
She went for a walk down the garden path

as she walked, she heard her love laugh.

She wasn't lonely now, she was with him in the

garden once more.

They found her today, beside the roses.

The smile on her face looked like she was posing.

They will bury her tomorrow in her dress of green,

in the garden beside of him.

THE FAMILY REUNION

The invitations were sent to all saying, come
join us if you can. We'll meet at the park, there's
room for all the clan.
Bring your favorite food and a little extra to share.
We'll bring the main dish like we did last year.
We'll play games and swim in the creek, we can hike
but not before we eat. I know for sure that I would be
weak.
We will talk and talk and tell tall tales, show pictures
of the ones we love dear, talk of days of long ago,
times were better then you know.
The hostess will make a speech over her mike,
welcoming all back from their hike.

We'll sing and dance until the setting of the sun and we will eat again and hug everyone. We'll tell the hostess we had fun, hope we can do this again when the next summer comes.

A PICTURE IN A FRAME

A picture in a frame
is for all to see. Its
beauty is to show. She
sends pictures to all her
friends and one to her beau.
She wears many different
styles and many different
smiles as she comes and goes.
The picture she loves the most
is her picture on the cover of
the most "Beautiful Magazine."
She's wearing designer clothes
and her best pose, she is beautiful

on that cover. She bought a picture for her mother and one for her brother to show.

MY PAY

Pay day comes once a week,

for this day I can hardly wait.

I spend every dime. I go to the

bakery, I wine and I dine. I have

a great time.

The rent I pay, the groceries I

buy and a kite for my little neighbor

to fly. I place some in the basket at

church, give a dollar to the man on the

corner who said that "He's out of work."

I don't invest in the future. What will

become of me? All that I save is what

they take out of that check before it's signed.

It's like I said, "I spend every dime."

THE RAILROAD MAN

The tracks are silent now.
The trains are few. The
railroad man goes to the
station each day to see the
trains pass through.
He spent his life working and
riding the rails, he will tell
you about the car he worked
called "The U.S. Mail."
Times were good then,
but they did end. They gave
him a gold watch and chain
as they retired him.

GRANDMA'S ATTIC

In the attic of grandma's house is an old trunk ragged and torn, in the trunk are treasures of old, beautiful letters tied in ribbons of gold.

Pictures on tin of my kin, of beautiful women and handsome men, children with curls, you can't tell if they are boys or girls.

Little dried flowers between the pages of poems, a wedding dress that I tried on; the letters I read, mother loved someone, the poems she had a collection of.

A few pieces of gold in a blue velvet purse, a comb made of shells and a hat with feathers, high button shoes made of leather, and more letters from a different fellow.

All of these things I'll put away. I'll come again to grandma's attic to play, there's much more I want to see, there's another trunk that's locked with a key. I'll ask grandma to open it for me.

LAWN PARTY

I went to a lawn party
beside the river's edge.
I could remember the
days of old, when I
was young and my
hair was red.
They had a band,
they sang and danced,
an auctioneer to sell
their wares to earn money
for church repair.
The children played and
the old folks talked,

some said they came in

cars, some said they

came in trucks. They

were happy to be there.

All joined in the cakewalk.

"STREETS OF MADISON"

I walk the streets of Madison, my
home town. Houses big and white
and a yellow one there about,
smiles all over town. All looked
so happy, no sad to be found.
Children skipping and skating,
on the front porch a few people
swinging, a few antique shops
here and there and a vegetable
stand near the town square.
On the corner a cop carrying a big
stick, he was ready for any trouble
one may bring. He must have been

happy too, when I walked by I could hear him sing. "I Walk the Streets of Madison, My Home Town."

"NO RAIN"

Everywhere it's dry, the
grass crackles under foot
as you walk, the weather
report said, "No rain."
The sky is clear, the air is dry,
not a cloud can be seen. "No rain."
The sun is hot, you can't
get cool, you set in the shade
and you say, "No rain."
The water is low, you can't
swim and you can't float, you
can't canoe and you can't
boat, "No rain."

JIM'S JEANS

Jim wore his jeans of blue,
they had been washed a time
or two. They looked a little
white. You may say they had
faded, that didn't bother Jim,
he enjoyed wearing them.
His mother kept him clean.
Every night she washed those
blue jeans and Jim. Jim, she
tucked in bed, read him a story
and sang a hymn and they
prayed and thanked God for
blessing every man. Mother
prayed especially for Jim.

LIGHT

Moonlight and sunlight
there's always light. I
know there're dismal days
with rain and snow. Days
like these help the flowers
to grow.
Delight of things bright
starlight, lamplight and
candle light that glow in the
night all will light your way.
But.
There's a light that glows
and glows, it's the light

of God that you plant in
your soul.
This brings happiness in
your life and to all that
know God is Light, he
made all light you know.

PAPARAZZI

I have to take pictures
of all that glitters before they
split. They are always hiding,
they want you to seek and
sometime they tease you
by giving you a quick peek.
Some have titles, some are
movie stars, they own towns,
cities and property on Mars,
they live in castles, mansions and such.
They wear their tux and their
fine gowns, they are the beautiful
people we love to be around. It's

my job is to report the news of
their dress and with whom they are seen.
They are in their big cars and private
planes. Some are escorted by kings
and some by queens. The parties
they attend are extravagant and
grand. They are the envy of every man.
The pictures that you see on the news
stand, for these we make a bundle,
life is grand.

TIME

We traveled back in time
visiting old ruins and
drinking old wine.
I think of the past and
the future excavating,
building and restoring
all the while we are
growing, moving into
another century,
passing the modern
wonders of this time.
Research gives some
answers to things we

want to know, about
outer space, earth,
the ocean tide. How
men lived and how
men died.

READY

The leaves, gold, red, green and brown
pretty wildflowers along the streets of town
the beauty of the sun shining down on
everyone, sky blue, the air clear. I'm
glad to be living here.
The grain is gold, the cornstalks brown,
the pumpkins are orange upon the ground,
after these colors there comes another hue.
We bring in logs for our fire, the snow will
come. We don't care if it's cold, we got
ready for it months ago.
We have our fire to keep us warm, plenty
of harvest from the farm, enough to share

with everyone.

We bring out our music, while dad sits and grins, he's happy that the crops are in.

We will play and dance until to bed we must go. We will take our showers, say our prayers and wish for snow.

?

Do you know who I am?
I'm red, white and blue
have a top hat, stand tall
and I'm proud.
For peace we have toiled
in foreign lands and on
American soil.
I'm for freedom for all,
whatever color, creed
or race, for equal
opportunity and living space.
For free speech all over
the land, the right to vote

for a president and other

women and men.

Free to worship the God

we choose, to work and

earn fair pay, have care

for the young and the old

and, to help those who

are hungry and have no home.

We the people of the free

land, we have no questions,

we hear the band. We

salute you Uncle Sam

SHENANDOAH

I walked to the foot of the hill, there's an old stream that meanders along. I followed the stream through the field and woods, the stream had gotten wider as it flowed.

I sat on a rock remembering when my dad and I had walked before, then I walked once more, I came to a bridge painted red and on that bridge was a sign that read "Welcome to the Shenandoah."

I walked past a garden and a pond. That must have been part of a farm, there were ducks swimming about, a gazebo and some flower beds and another sign that read: "Bed and Breakfast Just Ahead". It was the place we had stayed before when we walked the banks of the Shenandoah.

THERE'S A CARNIVAL IN OUR TOWN

The carousel goes around and around, little cups up and down. Children making happy sounds, there's a carnival in our town.

The carousel gallops gracefully, beautiful colors, the head so still; more fun to ride than the Ferris wheel.

There're games of chance, prizes to be won, throwing darts and shooting guns. At every game I try my luck, for each chance it cost a buck.

Win or lose, it's fun to play. I'll miss the carnival when it moves away.

COME TO THE CRAFTER'S FAIR

Crafts on tables and hanging on lines, valentine with beautiful rhymes, photo booths and gifts divine, little dolls, beads and books, toy stoves where you can cook. There're tables with bears and tigers, Easter bunnies and flags to wave, fire trucks and baseball cards, buy some to keep and some to trade.

There're bells to ring and toy trains that whistle. They have lots of things to sell, they have them by the bushel.

Funny pink pigs and white and black cows, painted on wood sunny sun flowers, ornaments to hang and kitchen towels.

Come, enjoy the day. Shop, please do, buy one of everything, maybe two. The Crafter's Fair welcomes you.

WATERMELON TIME

Grandpa planted the seeds on time
they grew into a little vine, then he
planted them by the water's edge at
watermelon planting time.
We would watch and wait as we
worked them with a hoe. We
could see the little melons as they
began to grow.
We would pick and pull this fruit
from the vine. We ate everything
but the seeds and the rind.
Everything that was left was made
into watermelon wine.

PRIVATE FOR A MOMENT

To have an acre of my own, private for a moment. If I should hear shots ringing in the air, I would know someone is hunting the wild instead of hunting a man who may have killed someone's child.

I wouldn't mind the thunder, rain, cold winters snow or frosted window panes, if I could be free away from the city private for a minute.

To have my acre where I could walk and be free, my God and me, no music from the metro, horns or sirens, just the birds chirping and the streams flowing free.

This is the way that I would like my acre to be

and if I should wander, I know, back to my acre

I would go, private for a moment.

INQUIRING MIND

They worked in the hills today, digging old fossils, bones here and there the oldest bones found anywhere.

So many resources in our ground, gold, silver and copper by the pound. There's coal and some crude, little streams beneath the earth and other things beginning to birth.

We dig for relics of long ago, testing them to see how old, regardless of what man may disturb, this is the way we learn to protect and preserve. Since the beginning of time man has had an inquiring mind. Research will help one to grow and stories to tell when they are old.

NEW TOY

He was on a journey
his plane was new.
He loved its color of
silver and blue.
He decided to take a
spin to see what his
plane could do.
He flipped and whirled,
what a delight. He would
go home now get ready
for another flight.
He washed and he shined
and he washed it once more.

He gave it a little push across

the floor.

He loved his toy of silver and

blue. He would show his dad,

he could be a pilot too.

BETRAYED

They played their drums, a feast was planned.
The moon was full they were expecting the
white man.
White man will bring gifts from their land. Feast,
they did and trades were made. White man wanted
more.
Soon there would be war. Chief getting his braves
ready to fight.
White man paid the price with many lives but, they
stayed. Red man had been friendly and they paid.
Red man pushed on reservation where they live
betrayed.

STORMY WEATHER

The sky is getting dark, the trees are bending in the wind, loud rumbling in the distance, I must hurry. I take the child from his pallet on the floor, wrapping him warmly, as I move swiftly in the wind.

I take the child to the hills. We hide there when the storms blow. We feel safe beneath the cliff. The storms blow, the child cries but all is well.

I nurse the child and he sleeps. It's dark but, I must keep watch. I nod, waiting for the light of day and the storms to move away. The child nestled in my arms, my bosom for his pillow. He must feel safe, he sleeps and cries no more.

The storm ceases, the moon rises over the mountain. We won't have to wait for dawn. The moon will light our way home. The cliffs empty now waiting for another storm and our return.

YELLOW ROSE

They buried him in the garden near Brownstown Road, my little brother I never knew.

In the garden are many graves. I don't know where my brother lays. There's no marker at the head or foot. I've been there many times to look and I always see the yellow rose moving in the breeze. I wonder which grave may be his. Is it the one beneath the yellow rose where the yellow petals cover the ground and does he know when those yellow petals fall.

Brother every time I pass this way, I stop at the gate and say a prayer and I wonder if you are beneath the yellow rose and if you know when those yellow petals fall.

Each time I leave I can smell the yellow rose scent in the air. Are you saying goodbye or wanting me to stay awhile. While I linger I pick a yellow petal to put between the pages of my book and each time I see it, I wonder, are you beneath the yellow rose and if you know when those yellow petals fall.

POWER TO THE PEOPLE

A queen of beauty and a handsome

King

Education

Rich

A great couple to rule.

The nation is prosperous.

The people are happy.

The king's in his court.

The queen is off to her charity.

There's always an enemy

running free.

Gossip

Too much free time

Too many guns

People changing their minds.

Wanting to revolt,

they would like to have a vote.

They say it's time.

WHAT A CHORE, WAR

What a chore war,

what could be worse

this place is dark,

no light can I find

hiding in this shelter

built by friends of

mine.

They escaped to safety

but I'm stationed here

cold and alone, waiting

for what, I'm not sure.

I dare make contact

with my comrades, the

enemy may hear. I'm
not afraid to fight. It's
being alone I fear.

PRESIDENT OF THE USA

President of the USA
elected by the people.
A job made for a special
person.
Presides over our nation
welcoming all visitors from
far and near.
Our country he holds dear,
we must be peacemakers
and help all mankind be free.
We do criticize, that's human
you know. The ball is in his
court, let him throw.

WALKERS WALK ABOUT

Hammering, hammering, making way for the train
over land, through the tough terrain.
The men with sweat running down their backs,
building a track through Walkers Outback.
Walkers people think it's grand to have a train
coming through their land.
The train will pass over Walkers Bridge, up
Walkers Hill by the camps and lumber mills.
Passing Walkers Creek, there are sights to see,
graffiti on the rocks saying "J loves T."
People swimming under Walkers Bridge, kicking
and splashing, laughter ringing out. A fun place
to live, is Walkers Walk About.

PATROL

Every evening when the sun goes
down, she rides her horse through
the streets of town.
Everything's quiet but the sound
of the hooves galloping up and
down.
East to west she's on patrol. She
keeps the peace for young and old.

WASTED SUNSET

Sunset gold
lilies in bloom
another lonely afternoon,
have new shoes and
beautiful gown. I
should be dancing.
This sunset shouldn't be
wasted, if I could meet
someone, we could be
dancing.
Sharing, caring
having our own lilies
in bloom, watching

the setting of sun and

dancing.

SANTA

He lands on the roof
looking for the chimney.
Suit red, boots black
all of his reindeer
tied out back.
A bag of toys he
carries on his back
in a big black bag, we
call a sack.
The chimney's clean,
my stocking's hung
I baked lots of cookies
and I left Santa one.

I'M IN BLACK

She's in her red satin dress,
her hair piled high, smile big
and bright, me in black on
our prom night.
We laughed and danced all night,
in the morning I drove her home,
I gave her my mother's ring. We
got married in the summer rain, the
flowers were red, her dress white,
I wore black on our wedding night.
Today we celebrate our fiftieth
wedding anniversary, a party given
by our twins, for the wonderful years

that have been. She wears white
and I wear black,
remembering.

I'M GAME

The class was small, the professor
was kind.
I'm in love, but young. I finish
my class, graduated on time, that
professor stayed on my mind.
We see each other many times,
he's divorced, so that's fine.
Years are passing. I get a
friendship ring, so small,
but I'm game. I'm in love.
I hate my job. I want to be a stay
at home wife. The professor
doesn't ask. Years are passing.

He's retiring, he buys me a ring.
We will be wed in the spring.
I'll continue to work. He will be
home retired. What will I get?
Married. Part of my dream,
what a game.

THE WIND

The wind blows with great force
and can do much damage. It
whistles through the cracks in
your attic, making a mournful
sound, you think of ghost and
you fear.
A soft gale pushing your sail,
what joy you feel.
It can be gentle and wonderful
on a hot day when it moves the
heat away.
A feel of the wind against your
skin and in your hair sometimes

welcome, sometimes not.

You can hear the sound as it

blows your hat from block to block.

GYPSY SOUL

Dark eyes, tear drops falling down, hair brown, tied in ribbons, color bold, a gypsy I'm told, wearing much gold she might have stole.

She dances barefoot in her dress of crimson with it's belt of gold, she will read you palm telling you what your future holds.

You think you could love her but you know as she works the crowd her wagon is being packed getting ready to move to another town.

She a gypsy you know, she must move, she has a nomadic soul.

PLACE OF REST

I'm sitting on the bridge my
feet dangling down,
looking at the sand and
the fisherman.
Wildflowers are blooming,
the trees are full of buds. The
robin in the birch building
nest for her baby birds.
I hear music from the church
across the way, they're singing
and praising the Lord. I
couldn't find a better place
to rest. I know this was a
place planned by God.

RUN LITTLE DEER RUN

The deer swift on its feet
lives in the forest, in the
lush deep.
The huntsman has the little
deer in the sight of his big
gun.
The deer the innocent one
run, run.
Another hunter sees the little
deer run. He said to
himself "I will get this one."
He feels the thrill as
he shoots his gun.

Run, run little deer run.

Run to the forest that lush

and deep. Little deer be swift

on your feet, run, run.

LIST TO SANTA

Christmas cookies and collectable candles,
Christmas ornaments and stuffed animals,
you can order reindeer too, just fill out your
list and mail it to Santa.
We have teddy bears, dolls that cry and
reindeer, if you wind them they really can fly.
Don't forget the reason for this celebration.
We have the Bible and other books,
crosses on chains and plaques to hang, that
read "Celebrate Jesus, He's the King."
There are guns, fishing poles, candy canes
and diamond rings, all kinds of things that
you may ask Santa Claus to bring.

Fill out your list. You can't order too much.
If we don't have it, our elves will make it,
and put it in the big black bag so Santa can
bring it.
There are cakes, candy, gingerbread men,
bikes,
sleds, fuzzy puppies and kittens, the list is
long. Make your selection. Santa will bring
everything on time. Have his snack ready,
milk
and cookies will be just fine.

ABOUT THE AUTHOR

I was born in Charlottesville, Virginia. I grew up on a farm in the beautiful Greene County, Virginia near the famous Shenandoah National Park.

I am married. I have one son a beautiful daughter-in-law and two wonderful grandsons.

I am retired from AT&T Communications. I enjoy playing board games with the family, collecting Hummel figurines, plates, old dishes, books and STUFF also visits from family and friends, my pleasure is a musical and a box of chocolates.

www.ingramcontent.com/pod-product-compliance
Ingram Content Group UK Ltd.
Pitfield, Milton Keynes, MK11 3LW, UK
UKHW040017200726
13854UKWH00001B/244

9 780759 637818